MW00528341

Divine Mercy Chaplet
for the Sick and Dying

MARIAN PRESS
STOCKBRIDGE MA 01263

Eucharistic Apostles of The Divine Mercy
An Imprint of Marian Press
2011

Available from:
Marian Helpers Center
Stockbridge, MA 01263

Prayerline:1-800-804-3823
Orderline: 1-800-462-7426
Website: www.marian.org

Imprimi Potest:
Very Rev. Walter M. Dziordz, MIC, D Min
Provincial Superior
February 22, 1999

ISBN: 978-0-944203-44-6

Eucharistic Apostles of The Divine Mercy
10016 Park Place Avenue
Riverview, FL 33569
(877) 380-0727

For texts from the English Edition of *Diary of St. Maria Faustina Kowalska*

Nihil Obstat:
George H. Pearce, SM
Former Archbishop of Suva, Fiji

Imprimatur:
Joseph F. Maguire
Bishop of Springfield, MA
April 9, 1984

*The religious name of Saint Maria Faustina was Sr. Maria Faustina
of the Most Blessed Sacrament.
In the world, she was known as Helena Kowalska.*

Printed in the United States of America

Table of Contents

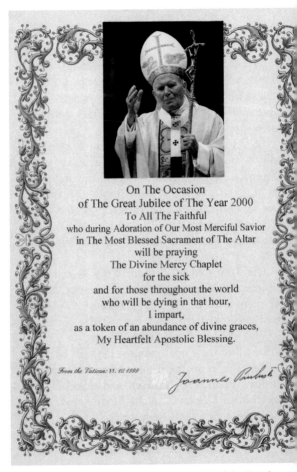

On The Occasion
of The Great Jubilee of The Year 2000
To All The Faithful
who during Adoration of Our Most Merciful Savior
in The Most Blessed Sacrament of The Altar
will be praying
The Divine Mercy Chaplet
for the sick
and for those throughout the world
who will be dying in that hour,
I impart,
as a token of an abundance of divine graces,
My Heartfelt Apostolic Blessing.

From the Vatican: 31. 10. 1999

Joannes Paulus II

(Participating chapels can receive a copy of the Papal
Blessing by contacting EADM at the address on page 2.)

Preface

Saint Maria Faustina records in her spiritual *Diary* Our Merciful Lord's conversation with a sinful soul. Jesus said, **"Behold, for you I have established a throne of mercy on earth — the tabernacle — and from this throne I desire to enter your heart"** (*Diary*, 1485).

Over 115,000 souls pass from this life each day: many do not know Jesus and most cannot get to the Tabernacle, let alone receive Holy Communion. By praying the Divine Mercy Chaplet before the Throne of Mercy in the presence of the Most Blessed Sacrament, for all those that are dying, we "are bringing mankind" (one dying soul at a time) "closer to" Jesus (*Diary*, 929).

Our Lord told St. Faustina: **Pray as much as you can for the dying. By your entreaties, obtain for them trust in My mercy, because they have most need of trust, and have it the least. Be assured that the grace of eternal salvation for certain souls in their final moment depends on your prayer. You know the whole abyss of My mercy, so draw upon it for yourself and especially for poor sinners. Sooner would heaven and earth turn into nothingness than would My mercy not embrace a trusting soul** (*Diary*, 1777).

May the zeal of Our Lord, Our Lady, and Saint Faustina for the salvation of souls inflame our hearts; and may this booklet serve to motivate us in this ministry so strongly encouraged by our Holy

Father, Pope John Paul II, who, on the occasion of the Jubilee Year, gave his Apostolic Blessing to all who will practice this spiritual work of mercy. For another way adorers might pray for the sick and dying during adoration using the Divine Mercy Chaplet, please see the optional prayer program in the Appendix, on page 41.

The Divine Mercy Chaplet

Recite on ordinary rosary beads (*Diary*, 476)

The Our Father

Our Father, who art in heaven, hallowed be Thy name; Thy kingdom come; Thy will be done on earth as it is in heaven. Give us this day our daily bread; and forgive us our trespasses as we forgive those who trespass against us; and lead us not into temptation, but deliver us from evil. Amen.

*The Hail Mary**

Hail Mary, full of grace. The Lord is with you. Blessed are you among women, and blessed is the fruit of your womb, Jesus. Holy Mary, Mother of God, pray for us sinners, now and at the hour of our death. Amen.

*The Apostles' Creed**

I believe in God, the Father almighty, Creator of heaven and earth, and in Jesus Christ, his only Son, our Lord, who was conceived by the Holy Spirit, born of the Virgin Mary, suffered under Pontius Pilate, was crucified, died, and was buried; he descended into hell; on the third day he rose again from the dead; he ascended into heaven, and is seated at the right hand of God the Father almighty; from there he will come to judge the living and the dead. I believe in the Holy Spirit, the holy catholic Church, the communion of saints, the forgiveness of sins, the resurrection of the body, and life everlasting. Amen.

On the "Our Father" beads:
(before each decade)

Eternal Father, I offer You the Body and Blood, Soul and Divinity of Your dearly beloved Son, Our Lord Jesus Christ, in atonement for our sins and those of the whole world.

On the "Hail Mary" beads:
(of each decade)

For the sake of His sorrowful Passion, have mercy on us and on the whole world.

Concluding Doxology:
(after five decades)

Holy God, Holy Mighty One, Holy Immortal One, have mercy on us and on the whole world. *(three times)*

Optional Concluding Prayer

Eternal God, in whom mercy is endless and the treasury of compassion inexhaustible, look kindly upon us and increase Your mercy in us, that in difficult moments we might not despair nor become despondent, but with great confidence submit ourselves to Your holy will, which is Love and Mercy itself *(Diary, 950)*.

*The wording of the Hail Mary complies with the translations of the U.S. Conference of Catholic Bishops. The wording of the Apostles' Creed conforms with the Roman Missal.

Why The Chaplet for the Sick and Dying?

"GOD AND SOULS" is the motto of Sister Maria Faustina of the Most Blessed Sacrament (in the world, Helena Kowalska). On the day of her beatification, Pope John Paul II quoted her as saying: "I clearly feel that my mission does not end with death, but begins." He added: "And it truly did! Her mission continues and is yielding astonishing fruit. It is truly marvelous how her devotion to the Merciful Jesus is spreading in our contemporary world and gaining so many human hearts! This is doubtlessly a sign of the times — a sign of our 20th Century."

One of the elements of the devotion that Jesus desired Saint Faustina to spread is called the Divine Mercy Chaplet. He wants it to be offered especially for sinners and for the dying. Jesus is quoted in St. Faustina's spiritual Diary (which the Church recognizes as being "among the outstanding works of mystical literature") as saying:

Pray as much as you can for the dying. By your entreaties [that is, insistent prayers] **obtain trust in My mercy for them, because they have most need of trust, and have it the least. Be assured that the grace of eternal salvation for certain souls in their final moment depends on your prayer. You know the whole abyss of My mercy, so draw upon it for yourself and especially for poor sinners. Sooner**

would heaven and earth turn into nothingness than would My mercy not embrace a trusting soul (*Diary*, 1777).

Saint Faustina was often given the grace to know when a certain dying person desired or needed prayer; she would be alerted to the moment by the needy soul, by her Guardian Angel or by Our Lord Himself. At those times she would pray until she no longer felt the need to pray, or a sense of peace came upon her, or she learned that the person had died, or heard the soul say, "Thank You!" She wrote: "Oh, dying souls are in such great need of prayer! O Jesus, inspire souls to pray often for the dying (*Diary*, 1015).

One of the best means of assisting the dying is the one that Jesus revealed to St. Faustina and insisted that she use often — even continuously: The Divine Mercy Chaplet. Jesus said:

My daughter, encourage souls to say the chaplet I have given to you. It pleases Me to grant everything they ask of Me by saying the chaplet. ...Write that, when they say this chaplet in the presence of the dying, I will stand between My Father and the dying person, not as the just Judge but as the merciful Savior (*Diary*, 1541).

Earlier, Our Lord said to her:

At the hour of their death, I defend as My own glory every soul that will say this chaplet;

or, when others say it for a dying person, the **pardon is the same** (*Diary,* 811).

Unfathomable Mercy Envelopes the Soul

Saint Faustina comments: "Oh, if only everyone realized how great the Lord's mercy is and how much we all need that mercy, especially at that crucial hour!" She wrote these words upon hearing God the Father say within her: **When this chaplet is said by the bedside of a dying person, divine wrath is placated, unfathomable mercy envelopes the soul, and the very depths of My tender mercy are moved for the sake of the sorrowful Passion of My Son** (*Diary,* 811).

How grateful we should be to receive these words from God the Father Himself! He assures us by them, that divine wrath (or anger) is not the result of a changeable mood in Him against sinners. His attitude toward us can never be anything but fatherly love and compassion (even if sometimes it has to take the form of warning, discipline, or chastisement — see Hebrews 12:5-11). But divine wrath is God's relentless war against sin, wherever He encounters it, because sin is the cause of spiritual, and even physical, death, if it is not stopped or destroyed. We also need to understand this when we read the explanation Jesus gave to St. Faustina concerning the red and pale [transparent] rays (depicted on His Divine Mercy Image) which symbolize the Blood and Water that flowed from His pierced side. He declared: **These rays shield souls**

11

from the wrath of My Father. Happy is the one who will dwell in their shelter, for the just hand of God shall not lay hold of him — that is, whoever is under the protection of the grace of Baptism, of Reconciliation, and of the Eucharist cannot be harmed when God acts with a vengeance to destroy sin wherever He meets it. Holy Scripture makes it very clear that God does not desire the death of a sinner, but that the sinner be converted, and live! In the prophet Ezekiel, we read: "Say to them, 'As surely as I live, declares the Sovereign Lord, I take no pleasure in the death of the wicked, but rather that they turn from their [evil] ways and live.'" (33:11)

What if the Person Prays from a Distance?

In 1997, after hearing a homily on having the trust of a child, Paul Regan of Malden, MA, reflected on Jesus' magnificent promise that one could obtain mercy for the dying by means of praying the Divine Mercy Chaplet. He wondered if the promise were applicable if the intercessor [the person offering the prayer] was not physically present at the bedside of the dying persons. The following experience recorded in her Diary by St. Faustina answered his question. She wrote:

It sometimes happens that the dying person is in the second or third building away, yet for the spirit space does not exist. It sometimes happens that I know about a death occurring several hundred kilometers away. This has happened several times with regard to my family and relatives and also sisters in religion, and even souls whom I have not known during their lifetime (*Diary,* 835).

And again:

My contact with the dying is, just as it has been in the past, very close. I often accompany a person who is dying far away; but my greatest joy is when I see the promise of mercy fulfilled in these souls. The Lord is faithful: What He once ordains — He fulfills (*Diary,* 935).

Perpetual Adoration Chapel for the Sick and Dying

These words are particularly relevant for Eucharistic adorers. As a result of Paul's sharing these convictions with some friends, on January 18, 1998, the first Divine Mercy Perpetual Adoration Chapel for the Sick and the Dying was established at St. Agnes Parish in Chicago Heights, Illinois. On the occasion of the chapel's inauguration, the Holy Father, Pope John Paul II, by a personally signed parchment, imparted a special Apostolic Blessing "to all those who will there adore Our Most Merciful Savior present in the Most Holy Sacrament of the Altar and pray the Chaplet of The Divine Mercy every hour for the sick and for all who throughout the world will be dying in that hour."

To understand their great mission better, Eucharistic Apostles of The Divine Mercy must be very much aware of the Diary passage in which St. Faustina recounts a deeply mystical experience:

> + Holy Hour — Thursday. During this hour of prayer, Jesus allowed me to enter the Cenacle [the "Upper Room" where the Last Supper took place], and I was a witness to what happened there. However, I was most deeply moved when, before the Consecration, Jesus raised His eyes to heaven and entered into a mysterious conversation with His Father. It is only in eternity that we shall really understand that moment. His eyes were like two flames; His face was radiant, white as snow; His whole personage full of majesty; His soul full of longing. At the moment of Consecration love rested satiated — the sacrifice fully consummated. Now only the external ceremony of death will be carried out — the external destruction; the essence [of the sacrifice] is in the Cenacle. Never in my whole life had I understood this mystery so profoundly as during that hour of adoration. Oh, how ardently I desire that the whole world would come to know this unfathomable mystery! (*Diary*, 684).

We see from this mystical experience of St. Faustina that the institution of the Most Holy Sacrament of the Eucharist on Holy Thursday was not merely a symbolic rite joined to the sacrifice on the Cross, but the institution (the changing of bread into His Body and wine into His Blood by His almighty word) was an integral part of that sacrifice. By means of the institution Jesus offered Himself to the Father, and in this way He crystallized the meaning of His Passion and Resurrection.

The death on the Cross could be understood in so many ways! The voluntary character of Christ's offering appears fully in the institution of the Eucharist: Jesus gave Himself with His own hands. He gave Himself freely — He was not a helpless victim. The personal and total aspect of this self-offering appears all the more clearly: Jesus gave His Body and His Blood; the words of institution "This chalice is the New Covenant in My Blood" reveal the value of this personal offering. Without those words, we could have doubts.

The Meaning of the Passion

So, the institution of the Eucharist expresses the most profound and complete meaning of the Passion, namely that it is the sacrifice of the covenant between God and human beings. By means of His Sacrifice, Jesus made the perfect offering in propitiation for our sins: He took the total punishment for them upon Himself, (this is the reason the Son of God assumed human nature by being born of the Virgin Mary), and, by that loving act, He removed the offending object, sin, that was the obstacle to restoring our union with God; by His innocent death He destroyed the death brought on by sin.

Saint Faustina was given to understand this by means of a symbolic vision. She described it in this way:

> ... I saw a great radiance and, in the midst of it, God the Father. Between this radiance and the earth I saw Jesus, nailed to the Cross in such a way that when God wanted to look at the earth, He had to look through the wounds of Jesus. And I understood that it was for the sake of Jesus that God blesses the earth (*Diary,* 60).

In the Old Testament, the covenant sacrifice required the sprinkling of the blood of the victim upon the golden lid of the Ark of the Covenant in the Holy of Holies. Beneath that lid, called "the propitiatory" and "the mercy seat," there were kept the stone tablets of God's commandments, representing the law that was broken by sin. The blood of propitiation, or at-one-ment, covered the broken law, and permitted God to prevent sin from bearing its rotten fruit — death (James 1:15). Unlike the blood of Abel, that cried out to God from the ground on which it was spilled (see Genesis 4:10-11) and called down a curse upon Cain, the Blood of Jesus, sprinkled on His own body, a body that kept God's law perfectly and was offered in loving sacrifice for others, speaks a better word than the blood of Abel (see Hebrews 12:24), a word of pardon ("Father, forgive them ...") and of blessing ("Peace be with you!" — John 20:19 and 26).

But, how does the Blood of Jesus accomplish this

pardon and blessing in us? Through the Sacraments He instituted, initially by Baptism and Confirmation, and then especially by Holy Communion and Reconciliation (Penance, Confession). When blood courses through our body, it enters every cell, first it absorbs into itself the poisons built-up in it, and then leaves behind in each cell life-giving oxygen and nutrition. This is what the Blood of Jesus does in the members of His mystical Body (the believers that together make up His Church): It removes from them the deadly poison of sin and replenishes in them the blessing of divine grace.

Communion with God

So, by the institution of the Eucharist — the new Covenant Sacrifice in His own Blood — [Take, eat ... Take, drink ...] Jesus has become food and drink for us. His sacrifice for us, then, not only makes Him pleasing to God, but it is also profitable for us, for it places us in intimate communion with Him and, by means of Him, with God. It also places us in intimate communion among ourselves, because it is a matter here of a meal taken by all together. Everyone eating at the same table has this sense of communion between persons — of the acceptance of one another, of friendly and brotherly relations. The Eucharistic Banquet does this even more, for, as St. Paul teaches in his First Letter to the Corinthians, because there is one loaf, we, who are many, are one body;

17

for we all partake of the one loaf, which is the Body of Christ (10:17).

The Last Supper and the Cross Unite in Holy Mass

All of these dimensions of Christ's sacrifice are not manifested on Golgotha: there Jesus dies alone; His disciples have abandoned Him. So, without the Eucharist, His sacrifice on the Cross by itself would not explain its own marvelous efficacy and fruitfulness. What our Holy Masses do is render present both, the Supper and the Cross, at the same time, here and now. The Supper and the Cross complete and explain each other. They also put into action the priestly ministry of the whole People of God, for all the baptized are called to be "a royal priesthood" (1 Peter 2:9), to be ministers of the New Covenant (see 2 Corinthians 3:6), to put the Covenant into action in their own lives, and to introduce others to it.

In the light of all that is stated above, the following entry in St. Faustina's spiritual Diary takes on a special significance for Eucharistic adorers:

When I immersed myself in prayer and united myself with all the Masses that were being celebrated all over the world at that time, I implored God, for the sake of all these Holy Masses, to have mercy on the world and especially on poor sinners who were dying at that moment. At the same instant, I received an interior answer from God that a thousand souls had received grace through the prayerful mediation I had offered to God. We do not know the number of souls that is ours to save through our prayers and sacrifices; therefore, let us always pray for sinners (*Diary,* 1783).

Immersed in prayer, St. Faustina united herself to all the Masses celebrated all over the world at the same time. How could she do this?

We, who are constricted by space and time in this created universe, and see events as separated from each other, must learn to see things from God's perspective. The Letter to the Hebrews assures us that Christ offered Himself without spot to God through the eternal Spirit (Hebrews 9:14). This means that the sacrifice of Jesus was seen as accepted by God from His eternal vantage point on the world: The "eternal now," where everything for God is "present" (as St. Thomas Aquinas teaches us: God sees everything all at once, in a single glance — all the past, all the present, and all the future). This is why all Holy Masses, no matter at what hour and in what place they are celebrated, make present the one, all-sufficient sacrifice offered to God by Jesus once-for-all in the Cenacle and on the Cross. In other words, what is eternally "present" to God (the Cenacle and the Cross) is made present, here and now, to us, too, at the Mass. This is also why the one and only sacrifice of Christ obtained for us an eternal redemption, in that its merits and fruit can be applied to any place, person, or experience, and to any moment in time: past, present, and future.

Obtaining God's Mercy for Ourselves and for the Whole World.

We who belong to Christ can do this work of applying the effects of His eternal redemption to the needs of the world, and we are expected by Him to undertake this work as members of His Body. These are great truths which we must believe absolutely (without doubt or reservation) if we are to be adequately motivated to share zealously in this great work of our Merciful Lord. Indeed, this is a vital part of our mission as members of His royal priesthood: to share in the priestly ministry of Christ by offering up His sacrifice, in intercessory prayer, to obtain God's mercy for ourselves and the whole world. As we say in the Chaplet: "Eternal Father, I offer You the Body and Blood, Soul and Divinity of Your dearly beloved Son, Our Lord Jesus Christ, in atonement for our sins, and those of the whole world" (see 1 John 2:2).

The devout praying of the Chaplet is, therefore, an important work of the priestly People of God. As we read in the Letter to the Hebrews (10:14), "...by one offering He has made perfect forever (that is, consecrated — Fr. A. Van Hoye: *Structure and Message of The Epistle To The Hebrews*, p. 69) those who are being sanctified." This means that Christ communicated the priesthood to us who belong to Him. Priests are supposed to "offer ... sacrifices for sins" (Hebrews 5:1). In that same letter, we Christians are encouraged: "Therefore let us continually offer the sacrifice of praise to God, that is, the fruit of our lips, acknowledging His name" (13:15). So, as we pray the Chaplet — "For the sake of His sorrowful Passion, have mercy on us and on the whole world" — we are doing just that: offering our "sacrifice of praise" to the Lord for His all-encompassing, saving work, and "offering sacrifices for sins." In other words, when we are prayerfully asking the Father, on the basis of the sorrowful Passion of His Son, for mercy upon the whole world, we are, in effect, prayerfully extending the Church's ancient cry from the Mass. "Kyrie Eleison" — "Lord, have mercy!" — and applying it to the whole universe!

Be Apostles of Divine Mercy

Now we can see the overwhelming greatness of the Divine Mercy Chaplet, for by it we become united to Jesus in His once-for-all, all-sufficient sacrifice. On the basis of this sacrifice, we invoke God's mercy upon the whole of creation, asking for mercy upon all people, upon the unborn generations of mankind, as well as on those whose life here is ending or has already ended. Truly, the Chaplet asks for Divine Mercy upon all that makes up the Cosmos [the Universe], subhuman, human, and angelic!

Through the praying of the Chaplet, too, whether continuously or often, we fulfill the desire of the Holy Father, John Paul II, who on Mercy Sunday 1999 said to the faithful gathered in St. Peter's Square in Rome: "I warmly encourage you to be apostles of Divine Mercy, like [St.] Faustina

Kowalska, wherever you live and work." And we also unite ourselves to our dear Sister Faustina in the Merciful Savior, and share in her ardent passion for "God and Souls!" that gives great glory to the Father, the Son, and the Holy Spirit.

These words of Saint Faustina should encourage us in responding to the Holy Father's call: "My union with the dying is still as close as ever. Oh, how incomprehensible is God's mercy that the Lord allows me, by my unworthy prayer, to come to the aid of the dying. I try to be at the side of every dying person whenever I can. Have confidence in God, for He is good and inconceivable. His mercy surpasses our understanding" (*Diary*, 880).

Abiding in Christ through Adoration

On Holy Thursday 1999, in his letter to Priests, the Holy Father declared: "The Eucharistic Liturgy is a preeminent school of Christian prayer for the community. The Mass opens up a wide variety of possibilities for a sound pedagogy [art of teaching] of the spirit. One of these is adoration of the Blessed Sacrament, which is a natural prolongation of the Eucharistic celebration. Through adoration, the faithful can enjoy a particular experience of 'abiding' in the love of Christ (see John 15:9), entering ever more deeply into His filial relationship with the Father."

In his Holy Thursday Letter to Priests 1980, the Holy Father stated: "Adoration of Christ in this sacrament of love must find its expression in diverse forms of eucharistic devotions: personal prayer before the Blessed Sacrament, hours of adoration; short, prolonged, annual exposition. ... The encouraging and the deepening of eucharistic worship are proof of that authentic renewal that the Council gave itself for a goal, and they are its central point ... Jesus awaits us in this sacrament of love. Let's not be stingy with our time to go meet Him in faith-filled adoration and in contemplation full of faith."

Father Rainiero Cantalamessa, the Capuchin monk who preaches Advent and Lent retreats to the members of the Papal Household, notices that we are witnessing the rebirth of a deep need of Eucharistic adoration, of remaining, like Mary of Bethany, at the feet of the Master (see Luke 10:39). We are rediscovering that the Mystical Body of Christ, which is the Church, cannot be born and develop otherwise than around its real body, which is the Eucharist.

He goes on to say that it is in this sense we're saying that the Eucharist "makes" the Church by means of contemplation. As we remain calm and silent, possibly for a long period, before Jesus in the Sacrament, it is His wishes in our regard that are perceived, it is our own plans that are given up to make way for those of Christ; it is God's light that, little by little, penetrates into the heart and heals it again.

There happens something that reminds us of what happens on trees in the springtime, and that is, the process of photosynthesis. From the branches there bud forth little leaves that, at first, are very, very pale; but simply by being exposed to the light of the sun, they absorb oxygen, become green, and make the whole plant "breathe." Without those little leaves a tree would remain a dry trunk and would not be able to bring its fruit to maturity.

This is a symbol of Eucharistic souls; Eucharistic souls, by contemplating [looking with deep concentration on] "the Sun of Righteousness," Christ Jesus, "absorb" His Spirit and transmit Him to the whole big tree which is the Church; they are like so many little leaves that make the plant "breathe." In other words, it's what the Apostle Paul says when he writes in 2 Corinthians 3:18:

> But we all, with unveiled faces beholding [reflecting] the Lord's glory as in a mirror [in Greek the word has the sense of "contemplating"], are being transformed into the same image with ever-increasing glory, which comes from the Lord, who is the Spirit.

This contemplation of the Eucharistic Lord, radiating upon us with the rays of His mercy, likewise serves to purify the Church, and all the souls that compose her, so that He can present her to himself radiant, without stain or wrinkle or any other blemish, but holy and blameless (see Ephesians 5:27).

Purification through Adoration

In his catecheses on Purgatory (August 4, 1999), Pope John Paul II explained that, in order to enter into perfect communion with God, every trace of attachment to evil must be eliminated, every imperfection of the soul corrected. Purification must be complete, and indeed this is precisely what is meant by the Church's teaching on purgatory.

And he stated that in the New Testament Christ is presented as the intercessor who assumes the functions of high priest on the day of expiation (see Hebrews 5:7; 7:25), but that in Him the priesthood is presented in a new and definitive form. He enters the heavenly shrine once and for all, to intercede with God on our behalf (see Hebrews 9:23-26, especially, verse 24). He is both priest and "victim of expiation" for the sins of the whole world. In other words, He is the one who turns aside God's wrath, taking away our sins, and not only ours but also the sins of the whole world! (see 1 John 2:2). The words Our Lord dictated for the Divine Mercy Chaplet prayer precisely express this: "... in atonement for our sins, and those of the whole world!"

We need to pay attention, then, to what the Holy Father says next, that is:

> "Jesus, as the great intercessor who atones for us [at-one-ment, from its Hebrew derivative, means to hide from view the offending object and so to remove the obstacle to reconciliation], will fully reveal Himself at the end of our life

when He will express Himself with the offer of mercy, but also with the inevitable judgement for those who refuse the Father's love and forgiveness."

The Holy Father capsulizes in those words the consoling message we read in Saint Faustina's Diary, which offers to Eucharistic adorers powerful motivation for praying the Chaplet for the dying, namely:

I often attend upon the dying and through entreaties obtain trust in God's mercy for them, and I implore God for an abundance of divine grace, which is always victorious. God's mercy sometimes touches the sinner at the last moment in a wondrous and mysterious way. Outwardly, it seems as if everything were lost, but it is not so. The soul, illumined by a ray of God's powerful final grace, turns to God in the last moment with such a power of love that, in an instant, it receives from God forgiveness of sin and punishment, while outwardly it shows no sign either of repentance or of contrition, because souls [at that stage] no longer react to external things. Oh, how beyond comprehension is God's mercy! But — horror! — there are also souls who voluntarily and consciously reject and scorn this grace! Although a person is at the point of death, the merciful God gives the soul that interior vivid moment, so that if the soul is willing, it has the possibility of returning to God. But sometimes, the obduracy in souls is so great that consciously they choose hell; they [thus] make useless all the prayers that other souls offer to God for them and even the efforts of God Himself (*Diary*, 1698).

Placing complete trust in God's unspeakably tender mercy, let us with Saint Faustina "implore God for an abundance of divine grace, which is always victorious." After all, Jesus told her:

The loss of each soul plunges Me into mortal sadness. You always console Me when you pray for sinners. The prayer most pleasing to Me is prayer for the conversion of sinners. Know, My daughter, that this prayer is always heard and answered (*Diary*, 1397).

Let us by our incessant praying of the Divine Mercy Chaplet hold the Good Lord to His word!

Eucharistic Adoration

In the Eucharist, Jesus offers His Body and Blood for spiritual growth, and grace to perform the duties of one's station in life. Any reading on Divine Mercy must include the Eucharist, as they are one and the same: The Divine Mercy Incarnate is Jesus, and Jesus is the Eucharist.

The Eucharist is one of the seven sacraments in the Church, and "The whole liturgical life of the Church revolves around the Eucharistic sacrifice and the sacraments" (*CCC*, 1113). "Sacraments are 'powers that come forth' from the Body of Christ, which is ever-living and life-giving. They are actions of the Holy Spirit at work in His Body, the Church" (*CCC*, 1116).

"The Holy Eucharist completes Christian initiation. Those who have been raised to the dignity of the royal priesthood by Baptism and configured more deeply to Christ by Confirmation participate with the whole community in the Lord's own sacrifice by means of the Eucharist" (*CCC*, 1322).

"The Eucharist is the source and summit of the Christian life. The other sacraments, and indeed all ecclesiastical ministries and works of the apostolate, are bound up with the Eucharist and are oriented toward it. For in the blessed Eucharist is contained the whole spiritual good of the Church, namely Christ Himself" (*CCC*, 1324).

Saint Faustina so loved the Eucharist that she added "of the Most Blessed Sacrament" to her name. She wrote,

"I find myself so weak that were it not for Holy Communion I would fall continually. One thing alone sustains me, and that is Holy Communion. From it I draw my strength; in it is all my comfort. I fear life on days when I do not receive Holy Communion. I fear my own self. Jesus concealed in the Host is everything to me. From the tabernacle I draw strength, power, courage, and light. Here, I seek consolation in time of anguish. I would not know how to give glory to God if I did not have the Eucharist in my heart" (*Diary*, 1037).

In The Divine Mercy Image, rays of Blood and Water emanate from the area of Jesus' pierced Heart, and Saint Faustina saw the same rays radiating from Our Eucharistic Lord in the monstrance. She wrote,

When I was in church waiting for confession, I saw the same rays issuing from the monstrance and spreading throughout the church. This lasted all through the service. After the Benediction, [the rays shone out] to both sides and returned again to the monstrance. Their appearance was bright and transparent like crystal. I asked Jesus that He deign to light the fire of His love in all souls that were cold. Beneath these rays a heart will grow warm even if it were like a block of ice; even if it were hard as a rock, it will crumble into dust (*Diary*, 370).

At another time she wrote,

> Once, the image was being exhibited over the altar during the Corpus Christi procession. [June 20, 1935]. When the priest exposed the Blessed Sacrament, and the choir began to sing, the rays from the image pierced the Sacred Host and spread out all over the world. Then I heard these words: **These rays of mercy will pass through you, just as they have passed through this Host, and they will go out through all the world**" (*Diary*, 441).

Not only are we to receive and adore the Eucharist, we must live the Eucharist. We are to let the rays of mercy from the monstrance pass through us and go out through all the world. We are to be icons of mercy, radiating love and mercy to others.

There is no greater way to energize ourselves to this task than by spending time in the Presence of the Source of Love and Mercy, Our Lord in the Most Holy Eucharist. This is seen in the example given by one saintly priest: If we were to sit for an hour a few feet away from a radioactive element, how much would that change and effect us? Now the Lord is infinitely more powerful than this and if we go to Him seeking His grace and mercy, how much more can we hope to be changed?!

Yet the Church distinguishes between the inherent, objective power of the Sacraments to confer grace as an action of Christ (*ex opere operato*) and the person's subjective disposition to receive that grace (*ex opere operantis*). Therefore, when at times it seems that our failings are too great and our faith too weak, we need to rely not on our feelings but put our faith into the fact of God's Presence.

In His infinite grace, God gives us that which we do not deserve and in His mercy, does not give us that which we do deserve. God has called us, despite our infidelity and lukewarmness, even more to Himself and by dozens of miracles of the Eucharist (a phrase, which is, in fact, redundant) has given irrefutable proofs of the Real Presence of Jesus in the Blessed Sacrament. The following are just three examples of these wonderful, generous gifts of the Almighty to a people undeserving.

Church-approved
Eucharistic Miracles

Lanciano, Italy

(700's)

Lanciano is a small coastal town on the Adriatic Sea. The word means "the lance," and tradition has it that Saint Longinus, the soldier whose lance pierced the heart of Jesus was from this town. Longinus converted after the events of the crucifixion and was eventually martyred for the faith.

At the time of this Eucharistic miracle, heresy was spreading in the Church regarding the Real Presence of Jesus in the Eucharist. A monk was having doubts that were growing stronger. One morning during Mass at the Consecration, he began to shake and tremble. He faced the people to show them what had happened.**The Host had turned to Flesh and the wine into Blood!**

The miracle took place nearly 1300 years ago and is ongoing. In the 1970s modern testing, including microscopic analysis, revealed the Flesh to be human heart tissue and the Blood of human origin, both AB blood type. There were no preservatives of any kind found in either specimen.

(Adapted with permission from *Eucharistic Miracles*, by Joan Cruz, 1987, Tan Books and Publishers. Picture used with permission of the Sanctuary of the Eucharistic Miracle.)

Santarém, Portugal

(1247)

A woman whose husband was unfaithful sought advice from a sorceress. The witch promised to help her if the woman would bring her a consecrated Host. Knowing this was wrong, she did as instructed.

She received Holy Communion but did not consume it. On the way to the sorceress, she noticed that the Host began to bleed. Fear overcame her, and she wrapped the Host in a veil and put it in a trunk in her home.

During the night, she and her husband were awakened by a bright light coming from the trunk which illuminated the room. The wife told her husband of the incident. Both spent the night on their knees in adoration. A priest was called and took the Host back to the church and sealed it in melted beeswax.

Nineteen years later, a priest opened the tabernacle and noticed the wax container had broken and the Host was sealed in a crystal pyx. The miracle is still celebrated with much festivity in Santarém, a city outside of Fatima.

(Adapted with permission from the *Study and Story of the Relics and Eucharistic Miracle of Santarém*, by Carlos Evaristo, 1992.)

Bagno di Romagna, Italy
(1412)

This Eucharistic miracle occurred in the small town of Bagno di Romagna as a priest was celebrating Holy Mass and doubting the True Presence of Our Lord in the Eucharist.

After consecrating the wine, he looked into the chalice and was shocked to see wine turned to Blood. It began to bubble out of the chalice and onto the corporal [altar cloth]. Shaken by the event, the priest prayed for forgiveness and lived with great devotion to Jesus in the Eucharist.

He has been given the title Venerable because of the pious life he led after the miracle.

In 1958, an investigation confirmed the corporal contained human blood and still retained properties of blood nearly 600 years later.

Perhaps the Blood was bubbling to show us that Jesus is alive in the Eucharist. We reflect on how we need to change after receiving Him, letting Jesus become alive in us and filling us with the power of the Holy Spirit.

(Adapted with permission from *Eucharistic Miracles*, by Joan Cruz, 1987, Tan Books and Publishers. Picture used with permission of the Parish of St. Mary of the Assumption, Msgr. Alfiero Rossi.)

Appendix:
Optional Adoration Prayer Program

I. Intention of Prayer Program

For the sick, suffering and all who will die today especially those unprepared for death.

II. Prayer for Souls in Need

Eternal Father, I offer You the most Precious Blood of Your Divine Son, Jesus, in union with the Masses said throughout the world today, for all the Holy Souls in Purgatory, for sinners everywhere, for sinners in the universal Church, those in my own home and within my family. Amen.

III. Litany of Reparation

Lord, have mercy on us.
  Christ, have mercy on us.
Lord, have mercy on us. Christ, hear us.
  Christ, graciously hear us.
God, the Father of Heaven, . . .   *have mercy on us.*
God the Son, Mediator between God and man,   " "
God the Holy Spirit, Enlightener of hearts,   " "
Holy and undivided Trinity,   " "
O Sacred Host! Victim of reparation for the
  sins of the world,   " "
O Sacred Host! Immolated on the altar for us
  and by us,   " "
O Sacred Host! Despised and neglected,   " "
O Sacred Host! Outraged by the blasphemies of
  men,   " "
O Sacred Host! Neglected and abandoned in
  Your temples,   " "

Be merciful unto us: *spare us, O Lord.*
Be merciful unto us: *hear us, O Lord.*

For so many unworthy Communions, . . .
we offer You our reparation, O Lord.
For the irreverence of Christians,   " "
For the continual blasphemies of the impious,   " "
For the infamous discourses made in Your holy
    temples,   " "
For the crimes of sinners,   " "
For the sacrileges which profane Your
    Sacrament of Love,   " "
For the coldness of Your children,   " "
For their contempt of Your loving invitations,   " "
For the infidelity of those who call them-
    selves Your friends,   " "
For the abuse of Your grace,   " "
For our unfaithfulness,   " "
For our delay in loving You,   " "
For our tepidity in Your holy service,   " "
For Your bitter sadness at the loss of souls,   " "
For Your long waiting at the door of our hearts, " "
For Your loving sighs,   " "
For Your loving tears,   " "
For Your loving imprisonment,   " "
For Your loving death,   " "

That You spare us, that You hear us, . . .
we sinners beseech You, hear us.
That You will make known Your love for us in
    this Most Holy Sacrament,   " "
That You will vouchsafe to accept our
    reparation, made in the spirit of humility,   " "

Lamb of God, You take away the sins of the world,
    spare us, O Lord.
Lamb of God, You take away the sins of the world,
    hear us, O Lord.
Lamb of God, You take away the sins of the world,
    have mercy on us, O Lord.

IV. Prayer of Reparation

Most Holy Trinity, Father, Son, and Holy Spirit, I adore You profoundly and I offer You the Most Precious Body, Blood, Soul and Divinity of Jesus Christ, present in all the tabernacles of the world, in reparation for the outrages, sacrileges and indifferences by which He is offended, and by the infinite merits of His Most Sacred Heart and through the Immaculate Heart of Mary, I beg the conversion of poor sinners.

V. An Act of Spiritual Communion

My Jesus, I believe that You are truly present in the Most Blessed Sacrament. I love You above all things, and I desire to possess You within my soul. Since I am unable now to receive You sacramentally, come at least spiritually into my heart. I embrace You as being already there, and unite myself wholly to You. Never permit me to be separated from You.

VI. The Divine Mercy Chaplet

Recite on ordinary rosary beads (*Diary*, 476)

The Our Father

Our Father, who art in heaven, hallowed be Thy name; Thy kingdom come; Thy will be done on earth as it is in heaven. Give us this day our daily bread; and forgive us our trespasses as we forgive those who trespass against us; and lead us not into temptation, but deliver us from evil. Amen.

*The Hail Mary**

Hail Mary, full of grace. The Lord is with you. Blessed are you among women, and blessed is the fruit of your womb, Jesus. Holy Mary, Mother of God, pray for us sinners, now and at the hour of our death. Amen.

*The Apostles' Creed**

I believe in God, the Father almighty, Creator of heaven and earth, and in Jesus Christ, his only Son, our Lord, who was conceived by the Holy Spirit, born of the Virgin Mary, suffered under Pontius Pilate, was crucified, died, and was buried; he descended into hell; on the third day he rose again from the dead; he ascended into heaven, and is seated at the right hand of God the Father almighty; from there he will come to judge the living and the dead. I believe in the Holy Spirit, the holy catholic Church, the communion of saints, the forgiveness of sins, the resurrection of the body, and life everlasting. Amen.

On the "Our Father" beads:
(before each decade)

Eternal Father, I offer You the Body and Blood, Soul and Divinity of Your dearly beloved Son, Our Lord Jesus Christ, in atonement for our sins and those of the whole world.

On the "Hail Mary" beads:
(of each decade)

For the sake of His sorrowful Passion, have mercy on us and on the whole world.

Concluding Doxology:
(after five decades)

Holy God, Holy Mighty One, Holy Immortal One, have mercy on us and on the whole world. *(three times)*

Optional Concluding Prayer

Eternal God, in whom mercy is endless and the treasury of compassion inexhaustible, look kindly upon us and increase Your mercy in us, that in difficult moments we might not despair nor become despondent, but with great confidence submit ourselves to Your holy will, which is Love and Mercy itself (*Diary*, 950).

VII. The Divine Praises

Blessed be God. Blessed be His Holy Name. Blessed be Jesus Christ, true God and true man. Blessed be the name of Jesus. Blessed be His most Sacred Heart. Blessed be His most Precious Blood. Blessed be Jesus in the most Holy Sacrament of the Altar. Blessed be the Holy Spirit, the Paraclete. Blessed be the great Mother of God, Mary most holy. Blessed be her holy and Immaculate Conception. Blessed be her glorious Assumption. Blessed be the name of Mary, virgin and mother. Blessed be St. Joseph her most chaste spouse. Blessed be God in His angels and in His saints.

VIII. Prayer for Divine Mercy

O Greatly Merciful God, Infinite Goodness, today all mankind calls out from the abyss of its misery to Your mercy—to Your compassion, O God; and it is with its mighty voice of misery that it cries out. Gracious God, do not reject the prayer of this earth's exiles! O Lord, Goodness beyond our understanding, who are acquainted with our misery through and through and know that by our own power we cannot ascend to You, we implore You, anticipate us with Your grace and keep on increasing Your mercy in us, that we may faithfully do Your Holy Will all through our life and at death's hour. Let the omnipotence of Your mercy shield us from the darts of our salvation's enemies, that we may with confidence, as Your children, await Your final coming—that day known to You alone. And we expect to obtain everything promised us by Jesus in spite of all our wretchedness. For Jesus is our Hope: Through His merciful Heart, as through an open gate, we pass through to heaven (*Diary*, 1570). Amen.

IX. Prayer to St. Joseph

O Saint Joseph, Foster Father of Jesus Christ and True Spouse of the Virgin Mary, pray for us and for those who will die this day (*or* night). Amen.

St. Joseph, Patron of the Dying

---

*The wording of the Hail Mary and the Apostles' Creed complies with the translations of the U.S. Conference of Catholic Bishops.

Eucharistic Apostles of The Divine Mercy

The Eucharistic Apostles of The Divine Mercy is building up the body of Christ through its worldwide network of Cenacles. This guided study program for prayer communities includes the study of Sacred Scripture, the *Catechism of the Catholic Church*, and the *Diary of St. Faustina*. The apostolate also promotes Eucharistic Adoration, together with hourly praying of The Divine Mercy Chaplet for the sick and dying.

For more information, call 1-877-380-0727
or e-mail: EADM@marian.org
www.thedivinemercy.org/EADM

MISSION STATEMENT
The Eucharistic Apostles
of The Divine Mercy

1) To profess and proclaim the truth of the Real Presence of Jesus in the Most Holy Eucharist, and to promote, insofar as possible, perpetual adoration of the Most Blessed Sacrament, and the hourly offering of The Divine Mercy Chaplet for the dying;

2) To bring the Divine Mercy message and devotion to a hurting world according to the revelations granted to the Church through Saint Faustina Kowalska;

3) To form small faith groups, called *cenacles*, which will meet weekly:

a) to pray for and encourage vocations to the priesthood and the religious life;

b) to pray and work for an end to the scourge of abortion in the world;

c) to experience the splendor of our Catholic Faith through the study of Sacred Scripture, the *Catechism of the Catholic Church* and the *Diary of Saint Maria Faustina Kowalska*;

4) To encourage members in the exercise of their Faith through the spiritual and corporal works of mercy; and to help people to become sensitive to the gift and the beauty of all life, especially through care for the "lepers" of today — the rejected, the lonely, the disabled, the elderly, and the dying.